About Distance

About Distance

Poems by Gregory Djanikian

Carnegie Mellon University Press
Pittsburgh 1995

Acknowledgments

Grateful acknowledgement is made to the editors of the following magazines in which these poems first appeared: *The American Scholar:* "About Distance," "A Moment for Husband and Wife"; *Antioch Review:* "At Stanley Bay"; *Ararat:* "Uncle Karekin," "When I Am Away from my Children"; *The Beloit Poetry Journal:* "The Persistence of Zachary"; *Boulevard:* "Dark Quarrel"; *Cimarron Review:* "The Teenager"; *Crazy Horse:* "Visiting Irasburg, Vermont in July," "Mrs. Mitstifer"; *Graham House Review:* "My Father Teaches Me A Kind of Driving"; *Gulf Stream Magazine:* "Uncle Hagop the Spendthrift," "Somewhere Between"; *Negative Capability:* "Grandmother, Garlic, and Alexandria"; *Poet Lore:* "Shooting Star"; *Poetry:* "Mrs. Caldera's House of Things," "The Visit," "In Alexandria"; *Poetry Northwest:* "Mrs. Kinsey's House of Children," "Unhappiness," "For Us"; *Raft:* "The Leap," "After Long Days of Rain"; *Tar River Poetry:* "Walking My Children Home from School"; *Yankee:* "In the New House."

"Grandmother, Garlic, and Alexandria" won the Rosalie Boyle award from the New England Poetry Club.

My thanks to the Corporation of Yaddo for two residencies during which some of these poems were written. Thanks also to Mark Halliday for his very helpful suggestions and to my wife, Alysa, who has been an invaluable first reader.

The Publication of this book is supported by grants from the National Endowment for the Arts in Washington, D.C., a Federal agency, and by the Pennsylvania Council on the Arts.

Library of Congress Catalog Number 94-70463
ISBN 0-88748-186-8
ISBN 0-88748-187-6 Pbk.

Contents

for my mother and father

I

In the New House

There is a dark mist above the ridge
of the next valley, the Black River.

The leaves of the Carolina poplar
are dancing furiously in the wind.

All over the hillside, animals
are becoming too heavy, folding down.

The children are deep in their rooms,
is it afternoon, is it morning?

My wife has been standing at the window,
Wherever I look, she says, *I am too new.*

The house is floating in the wind
in a reddish sea of uncut hay.

Three crows are cawing westward, a strange
light is tinting every clapboard of the barn.

There is a flash, a crack echoing
among the hills and suddenly

everything we have ever longed for
seems on the verge of arriving.

Visiting Irasburg, Vermont in July

We were drinking beer under the silver maple,
we were saying how lucky we were for awhile
to be out of the city where the temperature
had climbed to 102, cars had been stolen,
windows bashed, and people had begun to feel
their part of the world coming to some sort of end.
It was late afternoon, it had drizzled,
but now it was clearing, the wind was moving
through the trees making music, snaking
through the hayfields, Norman a half mile off
had been pounding his fence posts in
and Wayne Doncaster's cows were bellowing home.
We were saying this is where we ought to live,
just look at the space, never mind the long,
insane winter, look at our children
playing under the apple trees, and how calm
we've become, our desires are almost
comprehensible, we can almost touch them.
It was summer, and it had been hot,
there was a drought going on in the Midwest,
farmers had been losing their crops
and on the news the weatherman even here
was finding it more difficult to say
"Clear skies tomorrow," and we were sitting
under the silver maple, the late sun
filtering beautifully through the edges
of a cumulus cloud, and we were feeling
far enough removed from that kind of desperation—
last stands, suicides, huge, intangible
upheavals—to say, "This is the life."
It was late, we were going to get supper
on the table soon, but the sharp afternoon light
was so insistent against the hill behind us
that we stayed still hearing the shrill crows
in the white pines and Norman's sledgehammer
thudding and banging in the distance.
We were not going to think of the city

for awhile, of the neighbor beaten
in her house, intruders, alarms,
every noise the beginning of bad news.
We were going to call the children soon,
we were going to make some decisions,
everything was going to be all right.
Now two men we had never seen before
were walking along the dirt road
waving to us and we were waving back.
We could hear some boys in the high pasture
shouting and screaming, and a hammer finding
metal and clanging, and we were sitting
under the silver maple looking over Ware Creek
and across the fields toward the hillside
where faint smoke was rising off a barn roof,
and we were saying Steam, it must be,
steam, maybe a low cloud lifting,
maybe steam, we were saying, haze.

In the House Where Waiting Begins

The rugs are laid out like stepping stones,
the parlor windows are draped in thick damask,
and silence is settling
around each table leg, each armrest.

There is your aunt in the deepening chair
fingering the beads of her necklace.
Your uncle has been leaning
on the mantlepiece for how long?
Your mother, your sister, they are here,
and their hands have become
such small birds in their laps.

Upstairs, there is a soft exhalation—
is it your grandmother who has been sleeping
for too long, or the wind escaping
through the last open window,
or is it someone thinking just now
of a girl in a green frock years ago
with her hair bountifully unraveled?

How heavy things are becoming,
the floor lamp, the book of photographs,
the light fixture hanging densely from the ceiling
and causing what momentary tremors!

Outside in the breezy town
everything must be unloosening
and time has been floating away
like a flock of cumulus in the blue distance.

But how many days now
have the windows been opaque with evening?

How long since anyone
has lifted an arm,
or remembered to speak?

Mrs. Caldera's House of Things

You are sitting in Mrs. Caldera's kitchen,
you are sipping a glass of lemonade
and trying not to be too curious about
the box of plastic hummingbirds behind you,
the tray of tineless forks at your elbow.

You have heard about the backroom
where no one else has ever gone
and whatever enters, remains,
refrigerator doors, fused coils,
mower blades, milk bottles, pistons, gears.

"You never know," she says, rummaging
through a cedar chest of recipes,
"when something will come of use."

There is a vase of pencil tips on the table,
a bowl full of miniature wheels and axles.

Upstairs, where her children slept,
the doors will not close,
the stacks of magazines are burgeoning,
there are snow shoes and lampshades,
bedsprings and picture tubes,
and boxes and boxes of irreducibles!

You imagine the headline in the *Literalist Express*:
House Founders Under Weight Of Past.

But Mrs Caldera is baking cookies,
she is humming a song from childhood,
her arms are heavy and strong,
they have held babies, a husband,
tractor parts and gas tanks,
what have they not found a place for?

It is getting dark, you have sat for a long time.
If you move, you feel something will be disturbed,

there is room enough only for your body.
"Stay awhile," Mrs. Caldera says,
and never have you felt so valuable.

Mrs. Kinsey's House of Children

We are in Mrs. Kinsey's house
and it is full of farm children
dropped off each day, Martha and Noah,
Caleb and Abigail, too young
to drive cows or tractors, or cut hay.

Sometimes there are eight; today, eighteen.
The shy ones are in the corners looking tremulous,
the bold have claimed the best of the toys,
and Mrs. Kinsey is tending to all of them,
the bruised and fallen, the loutish and ever willful.

"Oh, they're good children," she says,
as she coaxes Eunice off her sister's chest,
or gently unlocks the arm around Erwin's head.
"Some need more than others," she says,
"and don't they have the harder time of it?"

Outside, Cyril is dangling from a branch
by one thin leg, Willy has pitched a stone,
and Helen is snagged in the raspberry bushes,
and Mrs Kinsey is trotting in and out
among the pandemonium of children,
retrieving strays and steering danger
away from heart and bone.

If, once, we could hear her shout
or ever see her raise an ugly hand,
we could say, yes, we know her limits now,
and aren't they much like ours?
Justice be served, we would say,
and the smallest crime find retribution.

But this is Mrs. Kinsey's house
where we are sitting and talking softly
and being our kindest selves all afternoon.
There are children all about us,

Adam and Sarah, Betty and Everett,
and Mrs. Kinsey is passing out crackers
and juice and pats on the head
to saints and villains alike.

"Maybe you'd like some too," she says,
turning our way, coming toward us,
and we are saying, "Thank you, thank you,"
along with Lara and Eben, Joshua and Rachel,
quietly, and all of us, for a moment, deserving,
in spite of what we may be, or might become.

Words for the Spare House

Even as he enters,
he feels he is the clutter,

the untucked shirt announcing him like a flag,
the ripe belly falling too languorously over his belt.

He wishes he had left his pocket change
on his bureau, he wishes he had foregone

the two sandwiches, the meaty tomato,
so much heaviness does he suddenly feel.

He jangles into the parlor.
He speaks, and already there is too much of him.

But where, he asks himself, are the casual snapshots,
the books waywardly shelved, the eccentric figurines?

Around him, all the table tops are rigorously clean,
all the gleaming counters are invincible:

everywhere he looks, there is more space
than he could ever hope to admire!

He breathes the minutest part of air.
He sits and becomes one of many quiet islands.

From every corner, his echo comes back to him,
Find me, it says, *find me if you can.*

The Visit

We had been sitting in his hospital room,
we knew it was cancer, we didn't know
how far it had traveled, what was involved,
but we had been talking for awhile,
we had settled into something almost comfortable,
what you could hear around the kitchen table,
maybe on a night out, or in a parking lot.
My uncle was lying in bed on his side
recovering from the spinal tap, the deep puncture,
my sister had been listing the features of her camera,
what crisp shots she could get with the slightest
adjustments, Hilary was telling us jokes,
the one about the lizard getting lucky,
striking oil, the one about the priest and rabbi
overturning in their car on slick ice,
and we were laughing, maybe a little harder
than was necessary, we were trying to convince ourselves
about something, maybe how unremarkable
all this was, maybe how we could keep it that way
if we said nothing risky, nothing about fear,
grief, love, nothing about time
or with the word *next* in it, next year, next week,
maybe then nothing would happen we thought,
we would walk out of the room and the world
would return itself to us as before, there, street,
there, house, there, lawn, there, bicycle.
My uncle was shifting and moving,
he was making some unaccountable noises
and we sat for an instant in a panic, very quiet,
very still, thinking always *morphine morphine*,
but he cleared his throat, asked one of us
to rearrange his pillow, fix the light
so it would fall on our faces, some simple thing
in an afternoon which was all but gone.
We heard a knock on the door, who is it this time
we thought, doctors, nurses? more bad news?
But it was someone passing out balloons

with *Nelson 8 yrs old* printed on each one,
someone was having a birthday on the ward,
we could imagine the cake, colored napkins, favors,
and what was a party without balloons,
and the remarkable thing was that we began
batting one around to each other, my uncle too,
his hand upraised, slapping at the balloon,
a faint smile beginning to play on his lips
and all of us thinking together, it must have been
together, *Keep it up, we'll be ok if we just
keep the damn thing floating.* "Uncle Jack," I said,
"you look just like a schoolboy, you look great."

Running through Arizona
for C. J. Bennett

You have never seen a saguaro before,
there have never been century plants in your life,
or yuccas, or prickly pear,

but you are running along them now,
on a dirt road, kicking up dust
through the cool morning air.

And you have never been as alert,
you have never needed to be,
except once in the heart of the city

when you turned and walked away
from someone who almost pulled his gun,
or in 7th grade when Frank Pulizzi

lowered his voice and whispered
"I'll get you after school," and all
you could think of in science was

the velocity of one fist against
your chin, and how you would have to run
faster than you ever had before,

and you are running now, making sure
there are no tarantulas, no scorpions underfoot, no lithe
mojave rattlers curling easily

toward the *pat pat pat* of your feet
in stride. Nocturnal here is what
you wish never to be, and even

running now at dawn seems ill-advised,
gila monsters still prowling for eggs perhaps,
or diamondbacks setting out from their nests

in any direction; and what about something

nearly domestic, that wayward bull for instance
looking up at you from the scrub grass, unpredictable,

half in love with moving targets.
You hear a rattle of locusts and every cell in you
shoots up to attention; you hear gunshots on the ridge

and you think of mountain lions
headed your way. You want to turn back,
you want to announce to Arizona

you're just a tourist passing through
and you wish to remember your visit
with, please, nothing too permanent.

But your legs won't stop; they love
the adrenaline in their muscles,
love being legs, your whole body

tipping forward to the miles ahead
and the *danger danger* you keep swiveling
to find in the everywhere about you,

running with neither ranch house
nor car nor signpost around,
running because it has never been

easier for you to run, the way
you have to keep nimble now,
the way you have to keep saving your life.

About Distance

We had come out to sight constellations,
we had been looking for a long time
with chart and flashlight, some sense
of where we stood, the huge distances.

Anne was in the house reading,
my wife and kids were already asleep,
and we were having trouble with Delphinus,
Cygnus too, Draco had lost its tail,
half the sky could have been Pegasus.

"Mike," I said, "look, the Dipper,
Polaris, we could have something here."

It was dark except for the light
on Marcel Cotnoir's heifer barn.
Sometimes we could hear moos and bellows,
and the night before we had heard coyotes
(coyotes!) howling from one pasture to another.

"Mike," I said, "maybe it's this chart,
or maybe the Pleiades are really lost,
all these dots, Mike."

We had been looking with keen intent,
we had been trying to nail down a small piece
of the sky, and we had managed to say
the obligatory words like "steep" and "vast"
as new stars rose, others disappeared,
"vertiginous," we said, and finally, "geez."

Maybe we could have said other things,
something about the furthest star
or about the folly of longing too much,
but our necks were beginning to ache
and we found ourselves looking at the faint
line of trees on the ridge of the hill,

and further down, we could make out
rail fencing against the Cotnoir house,
and maybe the outline of something moving
under the mock orange by our roadside.
We could hear the cicadas plainly now,
we could hear the river talking to itself
and Anne's voice suddenly from the doorway
calling to us, though we had already

begun moving in·that direction,
already we were walking that way,
the house looming tall ahead,
balancing the sky on its spires,
and the two of us feeling the ground
lush and slippery under our feet
while the earth turned imperceptibly eastward,
and all around us, dog, snake, bear, fish, bird,
were wheeling in the woods and waters, deeply alive.

II

My Father Teaches Me a Kind of Driving

When the steering wheel of the Topolino
came off in my father's hands in 1956,
we were driving on Rue Fouad in Alexandria,
passing donkeys laden with water jugs
and bicycle riders with stacks
of flat bread teetering on their heads,
and as the car swerved through the traffic
almost hitting the coffee vendors and the hookah carts,
"Don't worry," my father called out
to his stunned passengers in the backseat
and managed to put the wheel back on its stem
and cracked a smile even before
my grandmother could cross herself, or my aunt
had invoked the names of our ancestors.

"Boghos," they later said from the refuge
of the church steps, "your cars are always
in such ruin, and you a grown man."

And what was I thinking of
when I found myself one day on his lap,
my hands gripping the steering wheel
and my father working the pedals,
urging me along the Mediterranean?
The sea looked enormous and tilted,
I was ready to be pitched into it.
"Papa," I said, "is it a good idea?"
He was beeping the horn, people
were waving, laughing easily,
"Why sure," he said, "look at all
the space, and aren't we happy?"

"Such foolhardiness," my grandfather said
when we got home full of stories,
"Boghos," he said, "a small boy like that."

And wasn't there a general shaking of heads
when once he had fallen asleep driving to Cairo
on the desert road, the car overturning,
pinning his arm under the roof for hours?
Or when the rear axle of his Humber
suddenly dropped on Rue Ahmed Shawky
to the consternation of two policemen
and one scrap-metal dealer on his way home?
"This is unlikely," my uncle had said.
"Boghos," my mother had added.

*

So when I thought of cars as a boy
I thought of my father keeping things
on the verge of falling apart,
and so years later, after we had come
to America and settled down, after my father
had found work and driven into the ground
a second-hand Buick and Plymouth, a '61 Mercury
and through it all built himself a business
making shipping racks for Ford, GM;
after the family splintered and he left for Detroit
and we could tell he was arriving for visits
by the clink and rattle of his pistons;
after we had almost come to blows as father and son;
after the business failed when he was fifty-four
and we said that's it, that's a life gone by,
and he said, "Why sure, what's the worst
that can happen?" and surprised us all
by starting another which took hold;
after several of his cars had rusted out;
after the patchings up, the truces, the coming
to terms, after all this,

                              it was not surprising
to find myself in his car again
driving him on balding tires
to Williamsport, Pa. where we'd first lived.
There was fog settling in the hollows,
the asphalt bit by bit was disappearing.
I glanced at my father, sixtyish now,
in his topcoat and fedora, half looking
out the window and half not,
and wondered what it meant to be riding here,
steering him in and out of danger
toward a town we were once younger in.
I felt the thin rubber whir below me,
I felt the beginning of some notion,
the old car, I was about to say, the sea,
but I heard two pops and felt the grinding
of metal on pavement and held firm
while the car veered to the shoulder
and stopped. "That was bad," I said,
bringing out the jack and two spare tires
he somehow had, "that was serious."
I could feel him behind me as I began
changing the tires, the lug nuts clinking like glass
into the hubcaps, I could feel him standing there
as he might have stood forty years ago by another car
with the angel of wreckage at his shoulder
and his life's expanse wildly before him.
Papa, I was about to say, I don't know,
we should be more careful, these urgings.
He was checking the damaged rims,
he was whistling a sharp downward note,
"That was good driving," he was saying,
"that was ok, why sure, that was fine."

*

We are standing now in front of my house.
It is a cloudless day and the wind
is making the tall grass move by the dirt road.
"These cars now," he says, "they ride
so smooth, you hardly know where you are,
power steering, power brakes, one touch and *pffft.*"
"Smooth is good," I say, "smooth is fine."
"For an egg, maybe," he says with a grin, putting on
his hat and climbing into his vintage Ford Torino, 1978.
Two hubcaps are missing, one headlight,
and when he leaves there is so much black smoke
from the burning oil, so much dust, that for a moment
I've lost him, three, four seconds,
until he breaks free of it further down
and I can see him waving in the way happy men wave,
his arm straight out, his fingers spread,
thrusting themselves out into the world
without ambiguity, seen
and accounted for even from afar.

In Alexandria

Mamaka, our great aunt, has been standing
a long time on the curb of Rue Farida
waiting to cross. She has been letting
the traffic pass, the Fiats and trucks,
the mule carts and listing buses,
and once in a while, a long American sedan
with its black roof and fins flaring out.

Mamaka, we say, how long must you take?
She is immovable, her grey hair
is pulled back in a bun, her dark cotton dress
is fluttering like water around her knees.

Mamaka, we say, we have appointments,
obligations, the children.

She looks this way and that,
the street is stretching out like a great chasm before her,
and there is no hope for any of us.

But maybe tomorrow there'll be
less time, we argue, more traffic.

The cars are whizzing noisily by,
two bicycles have crashed into each other,
there is flat bread and broken glass everywhere,
and Mamaka is still standing at the curb
with her hands tucked in front of her
waiting for wings on her shoes
or a gust of wind to blow her across.

Let us take her by the elbows, we think,
carry her over with her feet skimming
the pavement and dancing like a girl's.

"One more minute," she says,
"children, some little time."

Maybe something might shimmer on the other side,
someone might call out *welcome* from afar.
Mamaka, we say, like this, like this,
take one foot, then the other.
We are such dark clouds at her shoulder,
such overly solicitous attendants!

"Some little time," she says,
preening her hair, clasping
and unclasping her purse,
"just one more minute, children,"
and she will not budge.

Uncle Hagop the Spendthrift

He is wearing a white linen suit
and shoes of thinnest Italian leather.
He nods impeccably to this neighbor, that,
tips his Panama to the smiling ladies.
One might think he is rich
but he's all credit, his bankbook floats
like the lightest of balloons.

Look, he says, I could paper myself
with money, but nothing helps, one by one
the bills fly away like sweet singing birds.

His friends shake their heads
from their yachts, their four-car garages,
"You could be rich," they call out
as he passes, "ah, such a pity!"

And his wife, furrowed with worry,
can't help but day-long dream
of bank vaults and deposit boxes,
the steely contours of armored cars.

Now his mother, tapping his cheeks, says,
"Little wastrel, what can I do with you,"
as he fills her kitchen with begonias
and artichokes, coriander and saffron.

"A shame, a shame," his cousins whisper,
"what will it get him but misery?"

But through it all,
his scrap metal business keeps going,
his children are well-fed, the roof
of his house is colorful and tight.

Now imagine, he says, closing his eyes,
that water is falling through your hands.
And are they not cool and moist?

And is the ground not replenished?
He clicks his tongue and winks.
Really, he says, how can life love
a miser the way it loves me?

For him the merchant stores blaze open
until all hours, the finest
cloths are laid on cafe tables.

And when he strolls about town,
what a music wafts from one end to the other,
what a giving and taking precedes his arrival
and continues long after he's gone.

Uncle Karekin

It was not the pock-marked face,
the deep nicks we would finger and count,

or the gold incisor that gleamed
like a small sun in his mouth.

It was not the dancing, hey-hey!
the fingers clicking like insects,

it was not the tumbles, the widening smile,
the drink still held aloft like a beacon,

or the quick winks he gave to the wives
under the starchy scowls of our fathers,

but it was the way he cupped his hands
over half his face and slowly blew out

a long, low, mournful *hoooo*
of a steamship moving out to sea

that caught us up, made us say,
Take us, Uncle, take us to that place.

At Stanley Bay

Alexandria, 1954

When my grandfather came back
from his swim, battered this time
by the treacherous currents, the rocks
jutting out of the water like knives,

my sister and I sidled into his room
thinking the house too quiet
and saw him like a hurt beast
standing by his bed, naked, wet.

My grandmother was kneeling, toweling his calves,
my mother was mixing a poultice.
"Look at his bruises," my sister was whispering,
"and the veins like swollen rivers."

We kept inching toward him
while my grandmother daubed him with cream
and wound him in a bedsheet
and made him odder than any dream of him.
"Children," she said turning toward us,
"let him sleep, this is your grandfather."

We hurried away, having said
not a word to him, nor he to us,
though our eyes had never left his body
and we ached to touch him, brush
our fingertips along the webs of cuts
and discolorations in his pale skin.

All day we wished he would somehow rise
like a true ghost, the sheet ruffling in the drafts;
"Grandfather," we whispered at his closed door,
"come to us, bring us your stories,"

but when the last lights were put out that night
and the dark spread about us like a purple bruise
we wished we had never wished what we had,

every waft of wind had a rustle to it
and the sound of water was deep in our ears

and by morning, he had become for us
in his shut room the ghostliest of imaginings,
and keeping our distance, we waited
only for his door to suddenly swing forth
and reveal him standing either healed
and smiling and unstrange, or what seemed
likelier to us now, about to change our lives.

Grandmother, Garlic, and Alexandria

I knew when my grandmother was ill,
I knew it even before I entered her apartment
and the faint smell of garlic met me
and would linger in every room.

Mezamama, I would call out,
where are you, how is your health today?

Sometimes in her robe and slippers,
garlic tied to her jaw with handkerchiefs,
she looked like the war wounded in films
or the invalid in the marketplace
whose bandages, I thought, held him together.
"Only a toothache," she'd say, waving me off
toward the balcony for a while
from where I could see the tram tracks
and further off, the blue of Stanley Bay,
and all around me, roses,
geraniums, begonias, and a garden
of bunched garlic hanging down.

Once, I found her in bed
propped up against a bank of pillows
listening to the radio, there was news of
Nasser seizing the Suez, British tanks
and the French rolling toward it.
"Nothing to worry about," she said,
a bowl of garlic at her fingertips,
peeled cloves along her shoulder and breast,
"a muscle strain maybe, the hot weather."

What about a doctor, my father would suggest,
some medicine, a shot of vitamins even.
"Little fig," she'd whisper in my ear,
"remember me, and always eat what you love."

And on the day my family left for Lebanon
on our circuitous passage to America,
the ship about to pull away and my grandmother
waving to us from the docks in a blue hat,
I tried to imagine, peering over the railing,
losing her for a moment in the crowd,
how much garlic it would take
to ward off the evil of departure.
"Mezamama," we shouted, "we'll see you, *insh' Allah*."
She was throwing us kisses, calling to us
through the long blasts of the ship's horn,
and everywhere I turned, I smelled harbor and sea.

*

And how was it that years later, somewhere
in northern Vermont, maybe as far
from Alexandria as I have ever gotten,
I found myself slicing cloves of garlic,
fixing supper for my wife and children
and listening to the radio: Beirut,
beautiful lost city of crater and rubble,
had been shelled again, the West Bank
was in riots, Iraqi guns had slaughtered
another zealous wave of Irani boys.
It was all bad, unchanging, predictable.
But then, a brief reprieve from the world's hate
for itself with this last, odd, coincidental report:
that the pepperiness of garlic, its tang,
its sulfur, was found conclusively to make it
of all things a natural antibiotic.
Mezamama, I thought, as I had not
for a long time, her garlicky meat pies
taking shape before me, the eggplants,
the lambs and yogurt, the dolmas and lahmajoons.
And how inconceivable it suddenly seemed
that I should be standing now where I was,

hearing my children's laughter outside
whose fears did not include for the time being
car bombs and gas canisters and mortar.
Where was that other life I had abandoned
somewhere on a dim pier in Alexandria
from where my grandmother had waved
and called out her love and let us pass?

Soon my children would come in, flushed and alive.
What inexplicable upheavals, lucky or not,
would their lives hold, I wondered.
Tonight, I would begin telling them the stories
they had never heard because I had forgotten,
first about garlic, its strange pungency,
then about their great-grandfather in the Turkish interior
dodging a sword, escaping into a new life,
about Alexandria, the muezzin calling hauntingly from above,
and the grilled corn on the streets, the pots of beans,
and about Awad and Elize, Chaké and Mme. Yazgy.
The stories were flooding over me now
as I bent over the stove, the garlic
sizzling in the buttered skillet,
and the scent wafting easily through the kitchen
and now throughout the house room by room
where it would linger, I knew, as it had before,
deep into the night, and maybe even into morning,
like a slow passage, as on a journey worth taking.

III

Going Back

We have been cruising, half a block
at a time, my wife, my two children,
all morning, and I have been pointing out
unhurriedly and with some feeling
places of consequence, sacred places,
backyards, lush fields, garages, alleyways.
"There," I say, "by this big cottonwood,
that's where I dropped the fly ball, 1959."
"And in 1961," I say, "at this very corner,
Barry Sapolsky tripped me up with his gym bag."
My son has fallen asleep, my daughter
has been nodding "yes" indiscriminately
for the last half hour, and my wife
has the frozen, wide-eyed look of the undead.
"Maybe lunch," I say, though I'm making now
my fourth approach to Curtin Jr. High School,
yellow-bricked, large-windowed, gothic,
where Frank Marone preyed on our terror once
and Janice Lehman walked in beauty.
"Salute, everyone," I say, "salute,"
bringing my hand up to my brow as we pass
the gilded entrance, "This is where things
of importance happened," and I am pulling out
from under the car seat a photo album
of old school pictures, "Page 8," I say,
"Fred Decker, John Carlson by the bike rack,
Mr. Burkett...," and driving on, following
the invisible map before my eyes.
Now we are drifting toward my boyhood house
and I am showing my wife trellised porches,
bike routes, more than she'd care to see;
"Why this longing?" she says, "What about now,
the kids, our lives together, lunch, me?"
I give her a kiss and turn right on Cherry
and there in front of our eyes, barely changed,
is the house where all my memories converge.
"Look at the windows of my room," I say,

"see, there, the shadowy figure moving behind them?"
And before anyone can hope to answer,
I have grabbed my camera, I am snapping
pictures through the windshield, bricks,
dormers, railings, fences, streets, all
are falling thrall to my aim.
"We could be happy here," I say, putting
another roll of film in and beginning
to nose my car toward Bill Corson's house.
"Really, Daddy," my daughter says; "No chance,"
my wife tacks on, but all I'm hearing
is the crack of bats in the neighborhood lot
and Danny's pearl-handled cap gun going off
and the drone of bees around honeysuckle
and Dewey Waugh's gravelly voice
urging on his mower, and the sound
of wind in the cottonwoods is like water,
I am coasting, there is time for everything.

Mr. Levering Our Scoutmaster
Gives Me a Sense of Perspective

"Get the Big Picture," he said to us,
squinting wisely at the distance,
"you need the Big Picture, boys,
so look ahead of you always
and know what's coming,"
and the twenty or so of us in our troop,
knapsacked and in uniform, knee-socked
and gartered and shining with glory
were outward bound and already feeling
the camaraderie of those naively marching off
to war, or maybe toward the bear and timber snake
of our severest dream, or the wide rivers
which might float us out to sea.

The Big Picture, I kept reminding myself
as we hiked, struck for the first time
by its import, the huge, dioramic fact of it
when inexplicably

                          my foot fell through air
and suddenly lodged halfway into a hole,
my scouting companions holding their bellies
in laughter, and Mr. Levering running toward me,
asking me why, dammit, had I not seen the Big Picture
though I had, I had, and that's why
I hadn't seen the hole, and under his glare
I thought I was stuck forever.

That night, tucked in my sleeping bag
and hearing the fire crackle outside the tent
and an owl hoot its lone refrain,
I felt I had botched my future,
that the true knowledge Mr. Levering
had tried to pass down to me, the hard
nutshell of wisdom, I had somehow
lost, or cracked beyond saving.

Where was that gauzy middle distance
of a life free of humiliation?

I dreamt late at night of a road
retreating into mystery,
disappearing toward one inscrutable point.
"Ambush," I said as I awoke

but it was morning, the sun
was streaming down through a cathedral
of leaves, the songbirds were chorusing
and there was hope again for all of us.
We had lined up in file, we were walking
once more and focusing our eyes
on what was neither too far nor close,
but it wasn't long before my attention
wavered and I began counting the beads
of sweat forming on Howard Switzer's neck
as he puffed on, or saw how one
of Johnny Breon's shoulders dipped
lower than the other, and closed my eyes
to listen to the raucousness of how many insects
or smell the profusion of mint as we passed it,
and heard my name called out as if from on high
and woke from my daze to stumble headlong
into who else but Mr. Levering shaking his head
and muttering "Sweet crimeny," helpless
before the unlearned and irretrievable.

We had been taking the trail through the woods,
it was thick with maples, oak and paper birch.
Looking down, Mr. Levering began, "You can't see
the forest...the trees, even...." but mercifully
never finished, patted me on the head and said, "Let's go,"
maybe figuring I'd come to know
in time how to best save myself.
He was all for heading back to supper
and the sweet desserts of civilization,

and now I was all for following in reprieve,
trying to keep my balance for both our sakes
over gully and root branch and rock,
upright with vast intention, but tipping
quietly toward home, foot by careful foot.

Mrs. Mitstifer

We had heard rumors, older sisters, brothers
had survived, bringing out with them
stories of her which would make us say
under our breath, "Let me move away,
let me skip a year or crack my skull."

But, inexorably, we had come of age
to the sixth grade, and now
she was raging, someone had given her
the wrong answer, or forgotten a salutation,
or had been foolish enough to say,
"Yes, Mrs. Mitstifer, thank you, I'm satisfied
with my low grade, my lot in life."
"Thunder and Lightning," she was booming at us
in front of a dark sky of blackboards,
magnificently hefty, Teutonic, eternal,
"Thunder and Lightning," and we were bent
like thin reeds under her rain.

It was not all show, there had been acts
of terror, disappearances, Florence Smink,
who had lost her homework three days running,
had been exiled for the hour to Phys. Ed.,
John Desidero had guessed False instead of True
and was hauled by his good ear to the office,
and once, she had said, "Not a peep out of you,"
and of course, Franklin Smith had peeped
and was lost to us for the day.

Now she had zeroed in on Joey Scaife
who had mismanaged his nine times-table.
"Thunder and Lightning," she bellowed
once, twice, and was into her third when
somewhere between the "Thunder" and the "Lightning"
something moved in her mouth—was it her teeth
trying to pop out like a bar of soap?—
and stopped her short and a great storm

was suddenly in retreat and the morning
emptied out into a silence.

What had happened? In the cafeteria,
there was great rejoicing and speculation.
It was risky, Jack Talley said, to deal
in such weather, no one could get it right.
"It's just her teeth," Franklin laughed,
"she didn't use no glue." Power, said Fred Decker,
speaking, as always, over our heads,
it could turn unmanageable, loop
around and strike you down.

Whatever we thought, we knew
that something had come to a close,
that even if Mrs. Mitstifer should return
to her great oaths and summonings,
they would prove inconsequential, small
next to the memory of her movable teeth.
We were making jokes, ungenerous ones,
though we couldn't stop ourselves,
we were laughing, and something was slowly
being lost, the mystery of Mrs. Mitstifer
looming above us, operatic, huge,
without end or finitude, Mrs. Mitstifer
without limit, and our belief in that.

Walking My Children Home From School

It's my day to walk them home, oh yeah,
my son who sings heavy rap at seven,
my ten-year-old daughter who knows enough
about sex and drugs at least to say no:
we've left behind the smaller boys to fight
and spit out all the four-letter words,
we've threaded our way through perfume and breathless talk
of biceps and the hard rock-and-rollers of the month,
and when I think if my world were likewise
too much with me at their age,
all I see is Billy Corson in sixth grade
flipping me the finger with a grin and making me
wonder all day just what it meant.

But this afternoon: we're meandering through
what seems like an old photograph of America,
the small town news on every doorstep,
porch swings drifting lazily in the breeze,
and someone waxing a '57 Chevy
maybe before the Big Date, and the radio tuned
to the Five Satins in the still of the night-to-be.

The pleasant limbo of walking home from school
ever the same: the homework deferred, bullies
and rumors survived, and the day for this brief
session of time, timeless and glossy.

It could almost remain for a while, this patina
of innocence, though there really is no Chevy
and little good news from the splintered world

but the wind is riffling through my daughter's hair
and my son is throwing acorns at all the trees
(just the pastoral quality of the word *acorns*!)
and I'm whistling "Teenager in Love" and thinking of
who else but Janine Metzger in junior high French
puckering her lips to say *toutes* and *oeuvre*.

Now a car rounds the corner too fast, squealing
its tires and disappearing into a driveway
and the noise is enough to shake me back
to my son pounding a stick against the sidewalk
and rapping out "humpety-hump uh-hunh," leaving me
to stumble over sweet Janine and *le temps perdu*,

and now my daughter down the block is asking me
what's holding me back, and I want to tell her
it's the worry of being overwhelmed, it's obligations
looming ahead, and the past suddenly
bearing more mystery than the future,

but what I do yell out to both of them is
"Careful," and "look both ways"
though already they've flashed a token glance
and are racing carelessly across the street,
their sneakers slapping against the hot asphalt.

Did the world ever stretch out as boldly
for us who now tend to them—brushing
their hair, washing them, making them ready—
always with some envy, envy, envy, god bless them?

Now I'm at the crosswalk: a couple holding hands
and spooning passes behind me—goodbye Janine, I think,
adios Bill Corson who first taught me the language
of the body. Cars are breezing by, gleaming
with possibility, there's a heavy back beat suddenly
playing on my fingers and a thrill shooting up my spine
as I step off the curb, making sure, for one moment,
I'm looking neither way, the road dizzying in the heat,
my children, from the other side, waving me on—

The Persistence of Zachary
for my son, age 7

Sometimes he's under his bed, or in the bathroom closet,
or wedged between the red couch and the wall.
He doesn't want to go to the dentist, doesn't like
his piano lessons or swimming class,
crouches behind the lush geranium, or poses
on the stereo speaker like a small statue.

Zachary, we say, we know where you are,
we've begun thinking like you, the space
under the coffee table, the dark hole
of the clothes hamper, how can you elude us?

Still he keeps trying, nabbed
in the kitchen cupboard among the brooms,
hauled off to school from out of the toy chest,
stoical, every disappearance
a brief rebellion against *have to* and *ought*.

What can we possibly tell him
that won't make us seem unbearably
correct and old-fogyish, betray
our love for this wild persistence?

Zach, boy, we call out hopefully
into the bureau drawers, the third-floor
crawl space, the shower stall,
reconfiguring the house in our minds,
all the good corners, the quirks, Zach, boy.

And tomorrow, late for an appointment,
how we'll threaten, cajole, and hate ourselves
as we force him out of the cellar perhaps
as though from an occult darkness
into the tamer light of our world.

It's bed time now and, mercifully,
he's under the right cover.

We read him a story, kiss him
goodnight, sweet dreams, we say,
then lumber downstairs to collapse
on the couch, our bodies plopped

against each other, and each of us thinking
how much our lives predictably will change
as *he* changes, or wondering how long
this incredible whimsy of his will go on,
or whether we want it to stop at all.

Compensations

My daughter, everyone says, looks
like my wife, though it's not true,
just look at the species of nose, I say,
the almond-shaped eyes, the slightly
quizzical slant of the mouth.

Everyone seems too polite,
this one nodding ambiguously at the ceiling,
that one leaving a trail of "hmm"'s in his wake
clinking like small faithless bells.

Oh, annoyance sometimes sticks me with its pin,
though I know it shouldn't matter,
this question of similitude, of connection.

But here I am bringing out the book
covered in green vellum, family snapshots
and some of my daughter laughing
by the juniper, or from the porch swing,
or standing now at the kitchen window
and staring toward some dark invisible cloud:
my eyes looking out of her eyes, I think,
my brow in her brow, her cheek, my cheek.
To be satisfied in this regard forever!

But why this desperate urge to prove
flesh of the flesh, I imagine my wife thinking,
why these claims, the subtle discernments?

What *am* I after? Something
like this incandescence which seeps now
from my daughter's bedroom,
lights my way up the stairs like a beacon?

And now she's opened her door: light floods
the hallway, "Daddy," she says,
"come sing to me," and how is it possible

not to deedle-dee-dee and sho-be-do
in her sanctum of dolls and enchantments?

And when I hit all the wrong notes
and her easy laughter falls about me
like a ring of flowers, how not to feel then
like an exile returning to the garden,
or a thief of breezy summer nights,
or a father whose child (his and not his)
loves in the only way she must know how:
without discretion, or purpose, or proof of requital.

The Teenager

She is a sullenness
ruling the upstairs hallway,
even light can't escape her,
and the house sinks
under the weight of her brooding.

Now we hear her rummaging
through her drawers, "Where is it?"
she is saying in a whirlwind
of impatience, "where is it?"
Shoes must be flying, maybe books,
the closet doors are banging back
and forth, and surely, we think, some law
of physics must be breaking down.

"All right," we say, "you need some space,
we know, we've been around."
She smiles almost too sweetly,
passes us by, the long trail
of her "no"'s winding darkly around us.

Even when she's out,
we are aware of our differences,
the locked room, the note left
as a boundary marker,
always this matter of limits.

Now we are at the kitchen table
watching her eat her salad,
one plateful, two, soon four,
why not the potatoes, we are about
to ask, why not the asparagus?
How easy to believe in *yes*, we think,
yes Algebra II, French in the subjunctive,
yes reason and cleanest laundry,
but the word trips heavily over her tongue,
falls back into the darkest maw.

"All right," we tell her, "we understand,
this is a war of nerves and ambushes,
this is a struggle for power,
tooth and nail, we remember."

Her face is as blank as a cloud,
("James Dean," we try, "Brando on a Harley,")
and when she blinks, she wipes away
the ancient history of our lives.

It's a stage, we say, this distancing
she's going through, this remaking,
a prelude for other changes,
we're fine, we say,
we might be going crazy, we say.

How is it time passes
so unbearably slowly, quickly?
Soon, with suitcases at our threshold,
she will be stepping over into her different lives
and we will be waving, giving her blessings.
This is peace, we'll soon be saying, this is contentment,
and the sky will be retrieving its familiar blue,
planets, stars, returning to their fixed orbits,
and our correctest selves will have come trudging back,
knocking heavily on our door again.

When I Am Away from my Children

But what dolorous music I must hear!
And my hair seems as grey as the sheeted sky.

Old one, I say to the mirror,
when will you make a final reckoning?
And my wife who must now be tending to them
in all their slipperiness
is getting younger by the beautiful minute!

Pistachios, I say to the waiter
(how my children love them)
ice cream with sauces, seconds
of everything, let me wake
to those other, bountiful days.

And when I'm strolling downtown
in a strange city,
or writing a poem in the room
with the open window

a child's wild cry may spring from the street
and I will abandon everything to it,
notebooks and music, the finest syllable,
could it be my daughter's, I'll think, or my son's?

Just the possibility of it!
The sheer, momentary desire
of seeing a face, before not seeing it.

IV

Shooting Star

They were lying down watching the night sky,
they were holding hands though they knew
they were straying in different directions,
"Andromeda," she was saying, but he was looking
at the serpent curling around itself.

They were in a clearing,
his skin was partly running along her skin,
but they had felt for awhile some unhappiness
creeping between them, she wanting this,
he doing that, and year after year
the unwieldy empire of domestic life.

They were alone, they were touching,
though if anyone else had been lying
with them—friend, lover, guest—
they might have turned to him,
"What can you tell us," they might have asked
in their desperately secret voices.

"Spica," she said, "Betelgeuse,"
he answered, "Deneb," and they knew
they were speaking in symbols,
pointing out different magnitudes of stars,
different configurations, carving up
this part of the sky, that part.

Was it too much habit, too much
the daily unbearable routine of themselves
which slanted one body away from the other?

Above them, the galaxy was spiraling upward
in all directions but all they could feel
was an almost falling through, this heaviness
of themselves against the ground,
this one palm pushing against another palm.

One of them was ready to rise and walk off,
one of them was about to say, "I'm tired"
in that familiar and accusing drawl
but somehow they were looking now at the same sky
and such was the light that blazed across it
as though Andromeda had been unchained
or Pegasus taken wing or Hercules
let fly his arrow that both called out
"shooting star" and were pleased to do so,
to see it together and name it incorrectly

which was really what they had been wishing for,
something serendipitous and wholly impossible
to pass through their lives, his body,
her body, the inexactitude suddenly
of their words coming together,
touching, if only for a moment, inexactly.

Somewhere Between

You are somewhere between happiness
and sadness, you don't know

where you are, but you think
that water is involved, and in fact,

you realize you've been floating
imperceptibly down a large river,

grey sheeted clouds above, and below,
the river bottom you haven't touched for days.

You remember the boat capsizing upstream,
or was there ever a boat, was there

just a falling in, and then this longing
to be carried without regret or hope.

The trees along the banks are barely moving,
the water itself is diaphanous, insubstantial.

And where, among rocks miles behind,
did you lodge your last thought of desire?

Now you feel the current slackening
against your fingertips (or is it picking up?),

now you hear a noise
coming from just around the bend,

and suddenly you can't tell whether
it sounds like hundreds of townspeople

clapping at news of your imminent arrival,
the feast about to begin,

or whether it's the waterfall
you've been drifting toward from the beginning,

the one without a name
but on all the maps.

Territories

They thought the trouble was over,
they thought they had talked it all out,
it was a mistake, she'd said, this infatuation
for someone else which had turned suddenly
too serious, she could see that now.

But they thought there was nothing left of it,
their nerves had been rubbed so raw
through bouts of anger, shame, even love,
so many words had come and gone between them
that they couldn't easily remember
what they'd said, what they'd imagined.

But it didn't matter now,
they thought they had gotten over
something difficult, something which had felt
immovable, the long unbearable ache
which had become too much a habit,
and they were celebrating in their way,
having dinner at a new expensive place
where they had no history of being together,
where they expected nothing.

They were sipping wine, a deep rich red,
the waiter was hovering over them like a generous uncle
and they were selecting everything he had suggested—
how good to be in his hands for awhile!

Soon it was happening, the old ardor
was coming back, they were beginning to flirt
with one another, the way she said *baby*,
the way his shoulder was brushing hers,
the way they were allowing themselves to think
for the first time in a long time
of the good sex they might later have,
the after-talk which would be easy and low.

And maybe he hadn't meant what he was about to say,
maybe when she remarked how she loved the leek soup
it was the wine in him, his jauntiness,
that made him ask what else she loved,
jokingly at first, whether she loved
the stuffed mushrooms on his plate, the braised beef,
or maybe she loved what others were having,
this one in the dark suit, or that one
with the coyly unbuttoned collar, or maybe
she loved the whole damn menu in fact,
he couldn't help himself, the words came
pouring forth, spilling all over the table.

And it was not until late at night
when she'd finally gone to her room
and closed herself off from him in sleep
that he stopped talking and remembered only half
of what he'd said because he'd said too much,
created too much damage, crossed some boundary
he had avoided most of his life.
Maybe it was desert, maybe tundra, or the white
insinuating madness of the polar ice cap,
but wherever he was was strange and dangerous,
and somehow dazzling for all that,
and only in the morning would he know for better or worse
in which direction each of them would be walking it,
though never had he felt, as he had tonight,
so permissive with himself, so luxuriously
tactless, having said again and again
the words he thought he could never bear
to use, so suddenly commonplace,
so readily available to him now.

A *Hill in Summer*

In the clear evening
a woman is standing on a hill
feeling along her bare arms
the heat of the sun diminish,
and the wind is ruffling her skirt
and swirling around her ankles.

Her children are asleep
in the house below,
perhaps her husband just now
is driving the backroads of another town
traveling toward her, or away.

She feels the wind play in her hair,
she feels the mossy, moist, cool
undergrowth cushion her feet,
and she knows no one else
will have this moment with her,
this life lived in secret.

She hears the soft tinkling of wind chimes
in the distance, feels the distance itself
receding and taking her along with it
toward the faint rosy wash of dusk,
the silhouette of far hills,
the pure light of ten thousand stars
suddenly appearing in the mind's clear spaces.

Oh, will no one stand behind her
neither to touch nor to comfort
but simply to witness with her
this steep falling away?

Soon she will gather her skirts
to turn and climb down as she must
though she will leave some part of her
still standing on that hill, calling
to be wild and dark and unraveled,

and no one but her will hear it
though it will seem fainter, further off
as house and child take her slowly in,
and the hill in its daily looming
will soon seem ordinary, and her hidden life
finally be hidden even from her,

in a world with many such lives,
and the wind full of voices.

Another Side

It has been going on for some days,
this call he makes at lunch, the coins
dropping into the slots with the sound

of tumblers clicking into place.
His voice is murmurous, almost as a lullaby,
the mouthpiece held delicately close, brushing

against the soft, secret flesh of his lips.
"Lilac," he whispers, "myrrh," he says, but he could say
anything, "carburetor" or "paper clip,"

and sound as allusive and full of touch.
But who is it that holds him so—new lover,
friend grown suddenly intimate, maybe the stranger

from his darker side he's always needed
to confess to, so much fastidiousness
in his life, so many neat folds and creases.

Say something, his wife might ask him
when he gets home, talk to me she may say,
and no doubt he'll tell her all about his day,

the entanglements, the enlargements of feeling,
despair, amusement, everything except
what he holds back, this dissonance,

the slight perturbations of his other life
which he now, even as he hangs the receiver up,
must hear without the machinery of thought

or afterthought, this noise in the ear,
this undercurrent which must go with him everywhere
and is always ready to betray him.

Unhappiness

It is an island—poor wretch!—
you might find yourself on,

dispossessed of almost
everything, even regret,

the crates of your belongings
bobbing horizonward like small goodbyes

and even your loved ones
winging away in the last rowboat.

Nothing now but this unbearable heat
you finally can't imagine your days without,

and once in a while, the wind-driven clouds
with their faint promise of *somewhere else.*

Soon this hopelessness you begin
relying on, how easy and poignant

to count the glass bottles
which somehow keep washing back,

to feel the island itself,
through tidal ebb and rise, slipping away.

Nothing beyond but sky blurring beautifully
into water, nothing but blue

into unerring blue, except, of course,
for the cruise ship suddenly heading your way,

billowing its white smoke
and blasting jubilance out of its horn,

which, now, you can make no sense of
and for which you can find no place

even though the gangplank is swinging down
and hundreds from the deck are shouting your name.

The Leap

He had never liked the cold, especially of water,
he had always loved the desert, the gusts
of dry wind, the disappearing horizons.

But he was standing now
along the bend of a small cold river,
the black willows drooping down,
lush meadows sloping to the carved edge,
and he was trying to decide which he preferred,
the heat of the sun on his shoulders
or the way the water gave back the light.

He was watching leaves drift in the current,
flicking downstream like delicate
paper boats of hope

and he was remembering how the woman
he had loved loved the coldness of rivers,
her taut naked body breaking the surface
and becoming for a moment the water itself
before her red-spangled hair shone through.

Now he had taken his shirt off,
he was sliding clumsily out of his pants,
his solar plexus tightening, a shudder
in the groin making him almost stupid.

He was going to go in, he knew it,
release himself from old allegiances,
the old lingering, complacent life betrayed:
he was arcing now into the question mark
he had always imagined he would come to,
the shape of his dive held just so,
perfectly suspended

before the first dark breathless icy blow
hit him on all sides, the onrushing
cold in every crevice, the current steepening,

and all he could do was try
to make himself as small and sleek a thing
as he could, swimming now for his life
which was what he had chosen to do
and everything was relying on his next breath,
everything he was or was going to become

on his reach, how far, how long
he could keep this pure instinctive desperate
burst of exhilaration going.

Dark Quarrel

It has been raining inside for days,
our ceilings are a grey unmoving stratus.

A criss-cross of rivulets was once window.
I look in the bedroom: marsh, I think.

It is a time for toadstool, fungus,
the month of the river rat.

When have we ever felt
so ill-fitted or out of place?

In the hallway, we pass each other
with such clumsiness, our bones bonier

from the chill that pelts us, hair Medusan:
where will such extravagance end?

Noah, I whisper, get thee from this place.
Rain, I say, go away truly.

I press my face to the window glass,
the landscape just beyond is shimmering

in a dream of fair weather,
and all we have to do, I know,

flinging everything open,
is walk out into it, like that,

though always through the doorway wide enough
for just one, and only then for the other.

The Sleeper

Something outside is rattling
in the breeze, some disturbance ready
to break the spell of morning
though it is still early
and the curtains are breathy with light.

Now for a long while
a man has been staring intently
along the whole ridge of a woman's body

and she has been sleeping without
awareness or attachment,
there is a smoothness in her brow
and her movements—the slender arms,
the thighs shifting under the sheets—
are languorous and slow: how easy
and predictable her breathing seems to him
and the day stretching out full of promise.

He wishes that the dark trailing clouds
would always turn wispy for them, he wishes
that happiness were as long-running
as a white picket fence,

but she is smiling now, undisturbed,
contented, as in a dream of a stranger lounging
on a red divan, whispering to her
something mysterious like *clavier* or *blue plum*
whose significance only she might know.

Soon the alarm will ring, or the crows
outside in the pines laugh derisively
as they often do, and the children rise
hungry for breakfast and tenderness.

Soon her eyes will open
to watch a man bend down to her kiss,

the same kiss every morning as if to say
I am and am not part of your life,

before the hour will sweep them both away
into their hundred disconnections,
these singular lives in the life together.

Now the woman turning in her sleep
toward the man, the man turned toward the woman,
these silences which hold, intersect.

Rara Avis

The first of summer and 4 a.m.
and there is a rustling beside me:
it is my wife, her pillow over her head,
her body shifting this way and that
and finding no comfort.

"The lousy birds," she says, and now,
because my attention has been diverted
(Gone the dream of lazy afternoons
and the sound of water in the trees!),
I hear them too, hundreds of them
in the cottonwood outside our open window,
singing like there's no tomorrow,
or because there is.

My wife throws off her sheets,
"Go away," she yells at them, "shoo,"
rattles the screens, hoots like a great horned owl,
but nothing happens, the profusion
of song continues, gets louder,
oppressive, she thinks, recurrent.

"Look," I say, "they're beautiful,
goldfinch, indigo bunting,
the wistful white-throated sparrow."

But it's not beauty she's after,
it's my old air rifle which she's found
and is shooting out the window,
hoping the pops will put the birds to flight,
but the trills are still there, the *chink*s and *heep*s,
the *whoit*s and *jeeaa*s and *tuk-tuk-tuk*s,
and now she's furiously retrieving
the noisemakers from our daughter's last birthday,
reloading our son's cap guns and taking aim,
the smoke of the burst powder rising
like fine incense above her head.

"Listen," I say, following her down
the stairs and out the door, "relax,
your blood pressure, the children,"
but she doesn't hear me, or doesn't want to,
she's all focus and tightened nerves,
("Rose-breasted grosbeak," I say,
"bluebirds flying over a rainbow"),
and she's picking up stones from the ground
and pitching them 50 feet into the larger branches,
and the birds are blithely chirruping,
crows are laughing from the high wires
and the stones are falling all around her.

"Look," I say over breakfast,
"I've never seen you like that,
this wild insistence almost beyond reason."
She waves me off with a smile,
tells me not to worry, she's been feeling
tired, hemmed in maybe, poor birds,
all she wanted was the world
held at bay for a while.
"It'll be better," she says, and kisses me,
and I do feel better, ready to do
the simple chores around the house
while she's off now to the market
to right the day and keep it balanced.

I see the shopping list she's forgotten
on the counter and the items read like a recipe
for easy and domestic life, except for one:
cereal, soap, milk, mortar shells,
eggs, bread. "Hold on," I call after her
not knowing if she's serious, "honeybunch,
sweetheart," but she's already revving up the motor
and, in a surge of power, tools down the road,
the chrome of her bumpers gleaming
like silver gunmetal, the birds oddly quiet,

and me waving the list like a telegram,
or a set of grievances, or my white flag
of surrender to her one-mindedness,
waiting for her to return with
who knows what else—sling shots, bazookas, chainsaws?—
half filled with terror, half mesmerized.

A *Moment for Husband and Wife*

To watch her painting an oil
of your garden, delphinium,
coral bell, foxglove and hollyhock.

To watch her standing in her white hat
beside the French easel, her wrist
bent just so, the brush lightly touching

canvas where now and again now
in dark blue, viridian, burnt umber,
flower and stem arrive and hold.

To be out of range of her seeing,
perhaps in the tall uncut grass
of the hillside behind,

peripheral, shadowy,
only a movement along the thin edge
of what does not contain you.

To feel her focus begin to narrow
and blaze on panicle or calyx,
whorled leaf or spike, her hand

barely moving, her eye fixed
only on the *there* of garden
and within the frame of garden retrieved.

To envy, then, the concentration,
enfolded, exclusionary,
all things around her falling off,

house, tree, hill, and grass,
and now you retreating quietly
toward kitchen or study,

forced to surrender the moment
to her, hers from the beginning
to shape, to be shaped by,

hers alone this attentiveness,
this fervor deep in the life
she keeps returning to you.

At Flood Time

We were canoeing on the Barton River
and feeling the eeriness
of being so high on the water.

Sometimes new stalks of corn or grass
speared through the surface
and there was no river,
it was marsh, it was a body
of water with no clear definition.

(You were wearing a red sleeveless blouse,
 the sun was freckling your shoulders.)

Upriver, we had spotted a bittern
standing still and pointing its beak
like a spire into the sky:
then its huge epiphanous lifting off
over the brimming water.

(There was the aroma of high summer,
 the air was charged with current.)

We were in the country trying to feel
expansive, though the night before
we'd heard our neighbors in a bad quarrel,
the accusations, the spate
of unforgivable words too familiar to us,
and something in their lives,
some innocence, coming to an end.

Look, you said, pointing
at a hay baler in two feet of water,
an island of ruin: we skimmed toward it
above the drowned grass and alfalfa,

such an excess of disaster
that we could say nothing
to encircle it.

(Later, we would think of the farmer
 talking low at his kitchen table,
 the zeroes accruing like bad cells.)

The wind was picking up now,
we saw bolts of lightning over the last hill
and thunderheads moving our way,

and soon we heard the crack, and the heavy rain
poured through leaf cover and fern, against canoe
and knapsack, *pokking* the water so hard
we couldn't hear ourselves, or tell
how far we'd gone over field markers
and fences laid flat, the lightning hitting
dangerously on all sides, beautiful, terrifying.

I knew we could never canoe this stretch again
without some disappointment, a longing
for the untamed upwelling of water,

though when I looked at you paddling
at the bow, your arms sculpted, straining
against the current, your back
like a fine tensile curve over river,

I felt thankful for lines of demarcation,
river banks for instance, or the thin
layer of fiberglass keeping us afloat,
or the lines of your body, elbow, hip,
singling you out from everything else
and allowing sometimes for a great wild
crossing over of them that is love.

After Long Days of Rain

The trees are singing again, the wind
is streaming through them with good current,

the white-throated sparrow is piercing
the late afternoon with its sharp clear whistle.

Look at the clouds, sun-bellied and cumulus,
sweeping along like a lovely idea of passage.

In the far acres, a farmer
is windrowing swaths of green hay

and the air is enlivened with its sweetness
and a deepening honeyed light.

And whose children swinging among apples,
and laughter burgeoning in the woods?

And soon it arrives again,
this nostalgia for just *what is*

even as one stands for a moment
with his life hanging open to it.

Now whatever else is to come—
heart's ache or ease—

to fill or bring down the day,
let it come simply and undisguised,

without high miracle or melodrama,
let it pass through here first.

For Us

Moonlight, and the cows are lowing
in the high pasture, and the Black River
is passing now under the bridge
that spans farm and farm.

And we are on that bridge
looking at the dark water flecked
with silver, momentary, elusive.
What makes us say, *This is beautiful?*

Fireflies are jeweling the woods,
the blackberries beyond are lush and dark,
still the sweet smell of cut hay rounds us
and the world is suddenly, briefly, ours.

And if I kissed you now,
wouldn't there be tremors through the wild roses,
nuances, quiverings in the aspen leaves?

And even if the moon were shining tonight
for a hundred lovers unfolding under the trees,
wouldn't we still whisper, *For us, for us?*